EXPECTATIONS ...
THEY'RE NOT IN THE
BIBLE!

Hop off the highway of expectations in your marriage and onto the road of respect.

Laura Provencio

WESTBOW
PRESS®
A DIVISION OF THOMAS NELSON
& ZONDERVAN

This book is a work of non-fiction. Unless otherwise noted, the author and the publisher make no explicit guarantees as to the accuracy of the information contained in this book and in some cases, names of people and places have been altered to protect their privacy.

WestBow Press books may be ordered through booksellers or by contacting:

WestBow Press
A Division of Thomas Nelson & Zondervan
1663 Liberty Drive
Bloomington, IN 47403
www.westbowpress.com
844-714-3454

Scripture quotations are from The ESV® Bible (The Holy Bible, English Standard Version®), copyright © 2001 by Crossway, a publishing ministry of Good News Publishers. Used by permission. All rights reserved.

ISBN: 978-1-6642-2761-3 (sc)
ISBN: 978-1-6642-2762-0 (e)

Library of Congress Control Number: 2021905287

Print information available on the last page.

WestBow Press rev. date: 03/17/2021

This book is dedicated to my prayer partner Audrey Rodriguez. Thank you for your prayers and encouragement to write another book!

Put on then, as God's chosen couple,
holy and beloved,
compassionate hearts, kindness,
humility, meekness, and patience,
bearing with one another and,
if one has a complaint against another,
forgiving each other.
as the Lord has forgiven you,
so you also must forgive.
And above all these put on love,
which binds everything together
in perfect harmony.
And let the peace of Christ
rule in your hearts,
to which indeed you were called
in one body.
And be thankful.

—Colossians 3:12–15

Contents

Preface

My husband and I were in premarital counseling when I heard for the first time in my life, "You should not have any expectations of your husband." What? Did that counselor even know what she was saying? How can you not have expectations of your spouse? There was a laundry list of things I expected my husband to do. Thankfully, that kind counselor spoke truth into my heart that day, and I decided right then and there that I would not have expectations in our marriage. That lasted for about six weeks!

This book is a medley of married life expectations, starting with my own, and adding the valuable input from family and friends. I was curious to see what expectations other wives had of their marriages and if they were biblically based, so I sent a questionnaire about expectations in marriage to my family and friends. Their responses gave me a fuller picture of what wives expect from their husbands and from marriage as a whole. Especially from women who have been married much longer than I have.

What I truly want to share with you is what the Bible says about marriage and how it encourages you to let go of expectations. Feel free to respect your husband so that you can live the abundant life that God designed for you. Marriage is marvelous when lived the way God created it to be.

Introduction

The idea of expectations is grounded so deeply into us, yet it is not mentioned in the Bible even once. There are commandments and directives in the Bible but not any expectations. We created those on our own. And the truth is, expectations are not from God. Yikes! This truth hurts, yet we need to hear it. Expectations creep into our hearts and minds like fleas. We don't know how they got there, but they are biting.

Where did these expectations come from exactly? Well, both my husband and I had different experiences in life before we met each other. We brought those experiences and prior knowledge into our marriage. Our ideas were formed by watching other married couples and hanging on to the things we wanted for our marriage, specifically, how I wanted him to treat me and how he wanted me to treat him. We both had expectations of how our marriage would look and feel from the moment we said, "I do."

For instance, I thought that all married couples held onto each other as they slept at night, and when they woke up in the morning, they were still clinging to each other. On my wedding night, we held each other close, but in the morning, we were at opposite sides of the bed. I wondered, *What does this mean?* and,

Do we still love each other if we roll apart while we sleep? Oh, the innocence of being newly married. I'm still giggling as I write this.

Or let's examine my husband's expectation of his proposal to me. He completely surprised me by proposing to me not only in public but in front of my future in-laws. My mouth literally dropped open as my handsome boyfriend got down on one knee. I was shocked! We had talked about getting married, but he said we had to date for two years first. He proposed to me after a year and a half of dating, and to my boyfriend's horror, I did not cry. I was in shock and awe. He asked me to make him the happiest man in the world, and I calmly said yes. His expectations were not met, and my now husband is still not over it. Hopefully in heaven he'll forgive me.

I want you to know that you are not alone on the expectations highway. I hope this book encourages you to get off your highway of expectations in marriage and onto the road of respect. Put down the list of what your husband isn't doing, and create in your heart the sacred love of togetherness. You got married for a reason. Make Jesus the center of your marriage because He has no expectations. He pours out His love to us so that we can love our spouses.

Chapter 1
Define Marriage

God did not plan for us to bring expectations of how things should be into marriage. From the minute God made man and woman, He said that they were good. God said that it's not good for man to be alone. A woman was created for a man (Genesis 2:18). God's goodness in marriage comes when a woman respects her husband and a husband loves his wife. God's directions for marriage are short and sweet and to the point. No expectations needed.

This is how "marriage" is defined in God's Word:

> Therefore, a man shall leave his father and his mother and hold fast to his wife and they shall become one flesh. (Genesis 2:24)

I really appreciate the action words in this verse. A man is to "leave" his parents and "hold fast to his wife." These are awesome attributes of a husband. Leave and cleave. Notice that God gives the directions to the husband. And my favorite part of this verse is that the husband and wife become one flesh. Ooh la la! God knows how to give good gifts!

In the very next chapter of Genesis, the first husband-and-wife team fall into sin. Why does sinning always seem to happen so fast? There are some serious consequences for all men and women because of Adam and Eve's sin. It's important we understand this so we can keep perspective on what marriage is and what God's consequences for original sin are.

To the woman He said, "I will surely multiply your pain in childbearing; in pain you shall bring forth children. Your desire shall be for your husband and he shall rule over you."

And to Adam He said,

> Because you have listened to the voice of your wife and have eaten of the tree of which I commanded you, "You shall not eat of it," cursed is the ground because of you; in pain you shall eat of it all the days of your life; thorns and thistles it shall bring forth for you; and you shall eat the plants of the field. By the sweat of your face you shall eat bread, till you return to the ground, for out of it you were taken; for you are dust, and to dust you shall return. (Genesis 3:16–19)

These major consequences should not be taken lightly. Let's look at the consequences for women. Childbirth will be insanely painful, and our husbands will rule over us even though we want to control them. Piece of cake! Not really. It's really hard to accept this. Especially since it's God's consequence for Eve's sin. Childbirth we can survive, but our husbands being in charge is a daily struggle. God gave us these consequences, not our husbands. They had nothing to do with it. Honest!

The consequence for men is that the ground they work is cursed. The work they do to provide for their families will require pain. They will have to sweat for their food and their families' food. Our husbands work hard at their jobs, and it can be a curse for them—or cause them to curse. This means that their consequence affects them every time they go to work. It's painful for our husbands to do their jobs and suffer these consequences daily.

Looking at the consequences of the first sin in Adam and Eve's marriage reveals to us that we enter marriage with some baggage. That baggage includes how we handle these God-given consequences. We should not put the blame on our husbands or add in our own expectations of them; the baggage we carry is our own. Thankfully, God's mercy on us is that we have the benefit of two becoming "one flesh." We endure the consequences of that first sin together.

God's Word will not pass away. (Amen to that!) We cannot change what God has said. His grace toward us is that we have His Holy Spirit to help us. We just need to pray and ask that His Holy Spirit will fill us and lead us. It's the same Holy Spirit that Jesus had. Jesus told His disciples that He had to ascend to heaven so that He could send the Holy Spirit to them. The Holy Spirit will strengthen us to face these consequences and lead us to victory.

Another section of scripture defines "marriage" as follows:

> However, let each one of you love his wife as himself and let the wife see that she respects her husband. (Ephesians 5:33)

Marriage is about love and respect, not expectations of each other. The husband is to love his wife, and the wife is to respect her husband. These action words define how we should behave toward our spouse. A husband is to love his wife prayerfully according to the wife's love language. A wife is to respect her husband by understanding that he is the God-ordained head of the household. Take a moment to reflect on this question: Are you showing these actions to your husband?

God has called each of us to have love and respect in our marriages, and God has good reasons for this. It's important to understand that we are ultimately working for the Lord. When husbands love their wives, they are serving the Lord. By respecting your husband, you are serving the Lord. Jesus, the perfect servant, left His example for us to follow. Obeying God in your marriage gives Him all the glory.

The Bible gives us yet another piece of wisdom about marriage in the following verse:

> Let marriage be held in honor among all, and let the marriage bed be undefiled, for God will judge the sexually immoral and adulterous. Keep your life free from the love of money, and be content with what you have, for he has said, "I will never leave you nor forsake you." (Hebrews 13:3–5)

Honoring your marriage above all else needs to become top priority in your life. Lift up your husband and honor him. You can honor your marriage by being fully committed to your spouse and not bringing anyone else into your bed. Faithfully commit to your marriage, and let go of expectations. I love the word "held" in this verse. Hold your marriage in honor, like a prized possession. Regard your marriage as worthy, and protect it from any fleeting temptations.

Following that first verse to honor your spouse faithfully are the words, "be content." Swallow that with a big gulp. Be content with what God has given to you. Be content with your husband, the amount of money God has provided for you, and understand that God will never leave you or forsake you. God has set you up for success in your marriage. Walk forward together in the confidence of the Lord.

To tell you the truth, I did not do this much research into God's definition of marriage before I got married. I knew the gist of what marriage was and that I wanted to be married for life. But the daily actions that go into a healthy marriage can only come from a prayerful heart. Women who have hearts and minds that first love the Lord and then love their husbands will have no room for expectations. This refresher on what marriage is from God's Word can guide us to make the necessary changes in our daily lives. God is for us, not against us.

Chapter 2
Newly Married

The wedding goes exactly as planned, or close enough, you officially say, "I do," and now you are ready to start marriage. You have a list of what you expect your husband to do for you, and you are ready for him to start with that one-hour back massage. You look across the room, and there is your one and only. The same person you've been dating but is now eternally bound to you. It's truly amazing! But a commitment lived out daily looks a lot different in real life than it does on Instagram or Facebook. Married life is not snapshots of your best pose; it's making dinner, doing dishes, and emptying the trash. Of course with a quick kiss in between.

Being newly married feels so fresh. You are both on your best behaviors and trying to put the other's needs above your own. It's marital bliss. The first year of marriage is also spent learning to compromise—compromise your ideas with your husband's ideas, your expectations and your husband's expectations—and learning which one of you is a night person and which one is a morning person. It's all the little details rolled into one beautiful life together. And a beautiful marriage sure is colorful!

Let's talk a little about learning to compromise. In truth, it never gets easier. Compromising our ideas of the way things should go in our marriage really can grate on us. Especially when you are newly married and trying to do the "right" thing. If you could let go of what you expect your husband to do, peace would reign in your heart. Compromise in daily life for the good of each other. If one of you feels more strongly about something than the other, compromise. If God is leading one of you down a new path and the other is resistant, pray. God will give you the ability to compromise in areas of your marriage that need unity.

The expectations you have for the beginning of your marriage seem so doable. You want your husband to make you happy. Then you find out that he uses Colgate toothpaste and you like Crest. And so begins the expectations. If he really loved you, he'd switch to Crest, right? It's the little details in married life that make all the difference. Release the expectations of what you want your husband to do, and love him for who he is.

Respecting your husband's needs above your own will start to work both ways. You just need to start the process by putting your husband's needs above your own. It's not his job; it's yours. You can only control your own behavior. God is in control of everything else. Start there. Do the things you can control in your marriage. For instance, your attitude, your tone, your ability to do the things you are good at. It's not your job to change your husband. That is God's job and in His timing. Be who you are, and this will benefit your spouse tremendously.

Your husband is not your idol. Nor is he your god. He is, according to the Bible, "the head of the wife even as Christ is the head of the church, his body, and is himself its Savior" (Ephesians 5:23). Christ is our Savior, and your husband is the leader of your marriage. A good leader is someone you want to follow. This is what God instructs through His Word. A husband leads his wife as Christ leads the church. This does not mean that your husband is Christ in your marriage or has to be exactly like Jesus. Your husband cannot save your soul. Stop expecting your spouse to be 100 percent Jesus in your marriage. Understand that you both need Jesus and His Holy Spirit in you to live out your marriage God's way.

Part of the two becoming one flesh means that both of your individual pieces and parts work best together—you being who you are in the Lord, and your husband being who he is in the Lord. You knew when you were dating exactly how your spouse behaved, and guess what, he is basically that same person. And technically, so are you. Now you're together in a marvelous marriage from God's point of view. Like peanut butter and jelly. One might be sticky and the other smooth, but together it's delicious!

A classic expectation when you're newly married is that your husband will be the spiritual leader that you want him to be. Biblically speaking, God says that the husband is the head of the wife. Your idea of what your husband should be doing as a spiritual leader is not an expectation from the Lord. God gave our husbands authority over us, which means they already have permission from God to have authority over our homes. They have what they need to be the spiritual leader, and whatever they may be lacking, God will provide. There is no description of what this looks like because all that matters is what God sees, not what you're expecting your husband to do.

Marriage is not an individual sport because you are now on the same team. You could even get matching jerseys! Being part of a team means you have to talk about your game plan. What are your goals in marriage? Are you doing what is best for your team? Having a team mentality will give you the proper perspective on your marriage and help you to do what is best for your marriage as a whole. Expectations do not help your team. "Fight the good fight of faith" (1 Timothy 6:12) in your marriage. You want your team to win!

In the beginning of your marriage you learn that sometimes the sweet one may have a little more spice that you didn't know about, and that the spicy one is actually quite sugary on the inside. This is what makes your marriage flavorful. The mix of two distinct personalities now living under the same roof creates a "signature blend" that defines your marriage. Don't expect that each of you has to do certain things. It takes time to figure out which one is good at cooking and which one manages finances well. Use your unique talents and abilities to create a marriage that is fulfilling and quite tasty.

Newly married life is the beginning of an adventurous journey. Being prepared for the long term requires that you pack the essentials. Expectations are not essential or necessary. Pack the things in your married life that you will need, such as love, joy, peace, and patience. Don't forget to add fun to the list! Enjoy the fact that your spouse was created for you. The richness of life together starts with a good foundation in the Lord. Pack and prepare for a lifetime of ups and downs and all arounds in your marriage. Know that God has a purpose for all of it. And the best part is it's all for your good!

Chapter 3
Kids

First comes love, then comes marriage, then comes baby in a baby carriage! Oh, the giant step into the unknown of becoming parents. This divine intervention can really shake up your marriage. If you thought buying a house together was hard, try parenting together. It puts a smile on my face thinking about what it was like becoming a mom and my husband becoming a dad. Expectations galore! Parenting adds a new dynamic to your marriage that really brings out the best and the worst of you. It's all out there now. Your true colors shine forth the minute your baby cries for the first time.

First you had expectations of your spouse as a husband, and now you add even more expectations on what it means to be a dad. And depending on how long you were married before you had your kids, the standards start building higher and higher. It's really a personality thing if you think about it. Your personality thinks things should go a certain way or not, and your husband either has similar beliefs or you're probably arguing every day. It's time to stop the madness. Reevaluate and appreciate each other. Parenting can be the great equalizer in your marriage.

Regarding parenting, you more than likely have the same beliefs on raising your child in God's way, but how you go about doing that is a whole other story. Each of you were raised in certain ways, and you bring that to your parenting. Now you are trying to figure out how you are going to raise your kids. Church once a week or twice a week? Pray before dinner or before bed or both? So many little details in how to raise your kids in God's way. Our expectations seem to get in the way of what God's ways really are.

This is the biblical definition of what God says about parenting: "Train up a child in the way he should go; even when he is old he will not depart from it" (Proverbs 22:6). That's all you have to do. Train your child in the way you and your husband believe they should go, and when your child is old, they will continue to do those things you trained them to do. That's it. It seems so simple, yet combining your expectations about training your kids along with your husband's expectations is not the easiest thing to do. Partnering in raising your children will give them the best of each of you.

Parenting your children together in your marriage will take a lifetime to work out. The spouse with the more dominating personality will probably put in the most effort to raise the kids a certain way or in a way they expect the kids should be raised. The other spouse will more than likely defer to the stronger ideals of "proper parenting," so to speak. We ultimately don't want to mess up our kids. Some parents like structure, while others go with the flow. Either way, you are raising your kids together. And don't forget that your children are watching your every move. You are your children's personal entertainment. Just try to keep it PG!

A helpful way to parent your kids is to make sure that your marriage is first priority. This important factor will really benefit your children and your marriage without any expectations. Everything you do as a parent has a ripple effect. When you hold your marriage above your parenting, you're being a godly example for your children. Remember the first line from the Ten Commandments is "God first." When you put God first, then your marriage, and then your kids, everything will fall into place. If you want to fit all the uneven rocks of your life in one vase, you must put the big rocks in first. Make sure you are prioritizing God and your marriage so that your whole family will be blessed.

Specific roles in a family are spelled out biblically with the words "love and respect." In marriage, wives are called to respect, and husbands are called to love. Whether your family has one working parent or two working parents, the words "love and respect" do not change. Do whatever God has directed your family to do. Don't lean on your personal expectations of how you want things to turn out. Lean on the truths of God's Word. Respect your husband so that the light of the Lord will shine through you.

The Bible is your tool to fight expectations in marriage. Use God's Word and win the battle of expectations within your heart. This way, when your kids are asking questions, you can go straight to the Bible for the answers. You are following God's Word by respecting your husband, so you can point your children to the guidebook of God's Word when they have questions. This is an extra bonus because your kids can't blame you; you are obeying the Lord.

Let's take a step back and think about how you were raised. Your experience, no matter good or bad, has an impact on how you are parenting your kids in the present. The awesome thing is when you have Jesus as your Lord and Savior, He guides your steps as you listen to Him. If you presently struggle with expectations in an area where you believe you were taught from your past, you can be freed from that behavior and walk in the new way that God has shown you. You can be the transition generation in your family that teaches your children God's way. And the best part of living your life for the Lord is that He is glorified as you raise your children. He has the victory in your life and your kids' lives.

Expecting perfection from your kids needs to be completely removed from your daily task list. Your children are not robots that you can program. "We destroy arguments and every lofty opinion raised against the knowledge of God and take every thought captive to obey Christ" (2 Corinthians 10:5). God has given you the official order to take your thoughts captive. Your thoughts only rule your mind because you let them. Stop expecting your kids to do the right thing every single time. They are kids. They need to make mistakes sometimes so that they can learn from them and learn to turn to the Lord. Just like we do.

God's purpose for your children's lives will prevail. We can trust that God is holding them in His hands and that He will work in their lives for good. We cannot put expectations on God to do things a certain way for our children. He knows what they need. "Children are a gift from the Lord" (Psalm 127:3). We need to guide them and let them be who they are in the Lord. God can be trusted 100 percent!

Your children were created with talents that God has future use for. Encourage your kids to use the gifts they have from God. Don't spend your precious years with your children expecting them to bend to your ways. Don't press them into your mold. Rather, hold them lightly as they are growing into what God created them to be. That way they can hear God's call on their lives and walk in that. Our God has great plans for our children, and we are just a small part of the magnificent process.

The pressure of parental expectations can be relieved by a simple addition problem: husband plus wife plus God equals peace. Use the tools from God's Word to define your parenting choices. Blend your unique ideas together by communicating in your marriage. Your family needs God as its center in order to thrive. Respecting your husband will move mountains in your family.

Chapter 4
The Seven-Year Itch

Your skin starts to feel dry. There's a funny feeling on the back of your neck. Something is really off. Then the itching starts. You look all over for the spot and just can't seem to find it. You look everywhere. Then you remember. It's the seven-year itch. Yep. Here you are in your marriage. You made it seven whole years, and some of your expectations have not been met. Bring on the ointment of God's truth to soothe your itchy soul.

Let's start with being honest. Married life is still the same after seven years. He still leaves the toilet seat up, and you still talk a lot during dinnertime. Those expectations of the little things changing over time have not changed. It's around this time that you feel a bit uncomfortable in your marriage. Probably because the person who needs to change is really you.

This is where the rubber meets the road. Those expectations you had about what your marriage would be or look like by now have possibly not happened, or things have changed in a way you never expected. You didn't know you'd be where you are still. You didn't know that your kids would be doing X, Y, and Z. Yet here you are at year 7, at a standstill. Questioning life, marriage, and what to do with that baby carriage that is still in the garage.

So this is married life. Some things are still rubbing you the wrong way, and other things are frustrating you. Some questions and/or expectations may be at the forefront of your mind. Why is my husband still the same? Why isn't he reading my mind by now? What about me? What am I doing with my life? Where are we going from here? Excellent questions that God's Word will answer. Go to the Bible, and let His Word comfort your soul.

This is the year that many marriages fail. The unmet expectations become too much, and heading for the hills looks very tempting. You need some hydrocortisone cream, and the answer looks like that nice man who listens to you at work. That other man is not the solution to your itch. "Therefore, what God has joined together, let not man separate" (Matthew 19:6). Jesus is the answer. Don't try to figure this out on your own. Go to the Source of life, and pray like you've never prayed before. Don't give up on your marriage. God will not give up on you.

When it comes to expectations, you have the preventive measures right in front of you. Go to God's Word. The salve of God's truth will relieve the pressure building inside you. Pour out the gunk of worldly ideas and solutions and fill up on the water that will never let you thirst again:

> Jesus said to her, "Everyone who drinks this water will be thirsty again, but whoever drinks the water that I will give him will never be thirsty again. The water that I will give him will become

in him a spring of water welling up to eternal life."
(John 4:13–14)

Drink in these words from the Bible. They are for building you up and giving you hope.

Think about a time when you tried to solve things in your own strength. Did it actually work? Probably not. Your expectations do not have the power to heal your marriage or your husband. Only the power of God can make any lasting changes in your marriage. "For God has not given us a spirit of fear, but of power and of love and of a sound mind" (2 Timothy 1:7). God gives us power and love and a sound mind. They are from Him. Any fears or frustrations are not from God. God gives us beneficial things for our times of need. If the time is now, take His offering of love. It will bless you abundantly.

You may be wondering what others are doing that looks like, "All's right with the world," within their marriage. That illusion is not true. Every couple has issues. There is no perfect marriage out there. "Perfect" should not be an expectation on the same line as "marriage." Let go of the, "He should be," expectations and face your reality. You married your husband, more than likely by choice. You want to be happily married. This can only happen through Jesus. Jesus will fill you with joy, and happiness will be the by-product.

For those naysayers out there who do not believe in the seven-year itch, you'll get itchy at some point. Don't dismiss this stage of marriage as only "those" couples who might need a little marital counseling. We all could use a little marriage counseling! The short course of premarital counseling may not be enough. It's really OK to talk to a third, neutral party when marriage issues cannot be resolved. Please talk to someone, and do not go down this road alone. We were never meant to be alone. We need each other!

Seven-year-itch expectations are not from God. And if it's not from God, it's probably not good at all. Let go of the expectations of who's right and who's wrong. Face the marriage struggles head-on, knowing that God is on your side. Cling to God's Word and pray together. Stay the course, and use the power of the true force—Jesus!

Chapter 5
Ten to Twenty Years

Roots. Deep roots. That is what comes to mind when I think of marriage in the ten- to twenty-year range. This is a season of marriage when your roots learn to go down deep to the Source, which is Jesus. This is the time of communicating the hard stuff and letting go of the expectations of each other. It's a time of crucial growth and a deepening of your relationship with your spouse. It is a time of possibly facing and growing through those hurts from early in marriage. The painful times actually strengthen your marriage. Without the dry seasons of life together, you wouldn't be compelled to seek the Lord. Either way, this time of daily grinds and routine is important for your marriage.

Think of all the dreams you had at the beginning of marriage. Some have come true, and others are still in the waiting stages. God knows. He has orchestrated every detail of your life. The nice part of being married is that you have each other to lean on during the trying times. You are in the thick of it together. Your kids are getting older, you are getting older, and your pets are getting older. Don't let go of the dreams you share as a couple.

Don't expect that things will never change or never happen. They will. All in good time, in God's time.

The strength you gain from going through life together gives you endurance and staying power. You may have expected that your husband should bring you happiness or that he should take care of everything. You know the truth now. Only God can bring you joy unspeakable. Those past expectations have come to light, and as you learn more about who you are in the Lord, you are changing. Those expectations are now unnecessary because God is filling your cup. The transition from looking to your husband for all your needs and now looking to Jesus brings a certain kind of beauty to your marriage. This feeling of dependency on the Lord replaces the expectations you put on your husband. Now you can enjoy marriage for what it is: a truly satisfying life together.

Communication, love, and honesty are what keep your marriage alive and well. You may have thought your husband could literally read your mind, but he needs your input. He needs your honesty spoken in love. This time of life, when facing trials of different sorts seems routine, you need the sounding board of your spouse. This is where the difficulty of being honest and really communicating comes into play. Having those hard conversations is not easy, but they are extremely beneficial to your marriage. Keeping the communication lines open is key to keeping the peace in your heart. Don't dig in your heels of expectation, but share your mind in a respectful way. Think about how you'd like to be treated, and treat your husband in that same way.

Your marriage vows were spoken before God and your family and friends. Those vows are important because sometimes you refer to them as you're hanging on by a thread. You committed yourself to your husband, and that was a vow before the Lord. "You shall be careful to do what has passed your lips, for you have voluntarily vowed to the Lord your God what you have promised with your mouth" (Deuteronomy 23:23). You promised to love and to cherish each other until death do you part, not until all your expectations are met. Think about what you vowed to your spouse and God. Take those vows seriously and live them daily. God will strengthen you to do what you promised.

Marriage is fun. Don't forget that! If you stopped having fun, start it up again. Go on that date night or take a dance class together. Do the things you enjoy doing together. Don't get caught up in the humdrum of life or stuck in old ways. Marriage was created by God, and His ways are very good. Don't forget to laugh and even giggle when need be. Be together in life. Marriage is not an isolated event or something that you may have expected to fade with time. If you need a spark in your life, ignite it with your husband. If you're "feeling it," then he will too.

Your husband knows you and you know him. Don't think that he doesn't know that you are going through something or that it doesn't affect him. It does. Share with your husband what you are going through so that he can try to understand or give you a break. If you don't share it, you can't expect him to miraculously know. If your husband is going through something, give him a break. He needs it! Understand that the hills and valleys of life are for our overall good, even if the current state of affairs seems overwhelming. Cling to the truth that you need to respect your husband. Ultimately you want what is best for both of you.

God gave you someone to lift you up and to be there for you in your marriage. Sometimes the expectations you have are not what you need. Trust that God gave you a husband who is good for you. Pray that you bring out the best of each other. Know that God's faithfulness to you is also that same faithfulness to your husband. "If God is for us, who can be against us?" (Romans 8:31). Who you are is beneficial for your husband and vice versa, whether it seems like it or not. In the good times and the bad, be there for each other. Don't let expectations dictate your behavior; love unconditionally through God's Holy Spirit. We need the Holy Spirit to help us to help each other.

Marriage is not only about us. Who we are as a couple affects our children, our extended families, friends, and strangers. God uses your marriage as an example to others. Imagine that! God also wants to show His love through you and your husband. Everyone is watching. Everyone. What kind of example are you being? Any expectations you had of your husband can easily be turned back to you. Love each other and understand that God brought you and your husband together for a reason. It's up to you how you respond.

This middle stage of marriage may have you feeling like the "middle child." Don't let that feeling get in the way of the truth that you have staying power in Jesus. You are learning to manage your spiritual growth together in your marriage. Don't yank your husband out of the ground or expect him to grow faster. Appreciate where God has each of you in life. Focus on what is in front of you and how you can be a respectful helpmate to him.

Overall, let your roots go down deep into God's Word, and

when the winds of circumstances blow, you are holding on strong to the Lord. "Two are better than one, because they have good reward for their toil. For if they fall, one will lift up his fellow" (Ecclesiastes 4:9–10). The two of you together are better than you by yourself. Think about how good it feels to stop your expectations of marriage and embrace what God meant for marriage. The seeds God planted in your heart will produce a harvest of His love when cultivated by His hands. Work together in your marriage, and reap the benefit of full blooms in the garden of your life.

Chapter 6
The Silver Anniversary

The silver anniversary (9,125 days to be exact) celebrates moments of memories during twenty-five years of marriage. Twenty-five years of sharing a bed, sharing meals, and sharing expectations. You've probably raised your kids and nearly paid off your mortgage. This is a life well lived together, including all the bumps and bruises along the way. Those challenges and uphill climbs only helped to solidify your commitment to each other. You are in this for the long haul, and your trailer is tailor-made!

You may expect more of the same after being married for twenty-five years, but find a new way to bond together. It's during this season that you have a big choice in front of you: Do you stay with the status quo, or do you start taking salsa lessons? After twenty-five years together you know all the nooks and crannies of your husband, and now might be the time to take that trip to Europe just to have a new place to take your luggage. It's time to remember what it was like dating your husband and start dating each other again. Expectations can be thrown out the window.

This new rediscovery of each other only adds to your marriage. Remember when you used to stay up all night talking, even though now you might stay up all night because of the late-night snacks you eat while watching Netflix. Don't let doldrums take over your marriage; create a new atmosphere of fun in your home. Don't let your expectations ruin your marriage. Step out in faith together and find an adventure to share. Communicate with each other about the possibility of fulfilling more of the items on your bucket list.

Staying committed through prayer is the backbone of letting go of expectations in your marriage. Prayer paves the way for peace and unity in your life together. Make time to pray together and spend time thanking God for His faithfulness. Remember that not only does God hear your prayers, He answers them in His perfect timing. Those prayers you prayed at the beginning of marriage may just be getting answered now:

> But do not overlook this one fact, beloved, that with the Lord one day is as a thousand years, and a thousand years as one day. The Lord is not slow to fulfill his promise as some count slowness, but is patient toward you, not wishing that any should perish, but that all should reach repentance. (2 Peter 3:8–9)

Your nest may be empty and expectations unfulfilled. You are making adjustments for your "new normal" as a couple now that the kids are gone from your family home. It's you and your husband full time now. This can be a good thing or a bad thing. Focus on the good. It's time to take that trip that has been on your mind for the last twenty-five years or to start a new hobby together. Give your marriage a "spa day" or start living your life "resort style." Fulfill some of those delayed dreams and do them together. Acknowledge that this time of life may feel awkward. It's OK. Embrace the change and hold on to each other. God will lead you into this next season of life in His wonderful ways. Have faith in Him.

For those of you who may feel like day-old bread, it's time to make lemonade out of those lemons! Spruce up your marriage with new activities and adventures. Or add a little spice to the coffee shop dates. You may have had expectations of what this time of marriage should look like or what your husband should have done by now. Only Jesus can change his heart. Pray and ask God to show you how to shake things up. God is the creator of all, including fun, so let Him be your cruise director.

Your marriage is important, and despite your differences of opinions, do something together! Don't let life slip away because you feel justified to stand by your expectations. Stick with the facts: You and your husband love each other, and your love has stood the test of time. You already know how good it can be, and if that is not your experience thus far, find the good. God will guide you every single time you look to Him.

Health issues can come into play during this phase of your marriage. "In sickness and in health" is a daily reality for you. Rolling your eyes at your husband is not advised but only because it doesn't solve anything. You need to support and respect your husband, and it might be time to kick in those caretaker skills. The best part is that when you lift up your husband with your words and at times physically with your hands, he will feel loved.

He will keep going even if his health is deteriorating. You are the one who will make a difference. You have purpose. God will be with you.

Let's talk a little bit about losing your memory after twenty-five years. Sometimes it can be a good thing. Maybe that grudge you were holding against your husband has been forgotten or not at the forefront of your mind as much as it once was. Your expectations may have changed a bit. We can take those thoughts that seem to dictate our behaviors and bring them to Jesus. He will lead the way to peace in your home. Don't let thoughts run wild and start the blame game. Bring your thoughts to the One who can make those changes in your life. The ripple effect will bless your husband as well.

The silver anniversary is one to be honored, especially because it's an honor to be married. The blessing of raising your kids and finding a new way to connect as a couple will continue to add years of bliss to your marriage. Expectations are not your primary way of communication, but living out God's Word in your marriage is fostering a home built on godly principles. Make your marriage your happy place.

Chapter 7
Till Death Do You Part

When you said, "I do," you also said, "Till death do you part." This was a promise you made to your husband. A commitment not dependent on your husband's behavior or personality but a commitment that you vowed before the Lord. Until death. That's a long time to love one another. Those expectations will cause tension to your one flesh, and this can negatively affect your one flesh. We do not want that! We want to honor our commitment to each other.

When you sit on the high horse of expectation, is this adding to your marriage or taking away? God is at work in you and in your husband. Until the day you die, God is in the process of refining you. The struggle in marriage lies in the truth that when God is pruning you, He may be blessing your husband. God teaches us individually in our relationship with Him. He is bringing us from glory to glory and hopefully not having to drag us there.

When looking from the perspective of being married for life, we need to change those expectations into realizations. Realize that God is Lord of your life and that He is in control of all things. "For my thoughts are not your thoughts, neither are your ways my ways, declares the Lord" (Isaiah 55:8). Realize that the commitment and respect that God created for your marriage are meant to be blessings, not curses. Understand that you need to be *for* your marriage and not against it.

God created us to live in the garden with Him forever, but our sinfulness changed His original plan. Sin can wreak havoc on a marriage when you don't acknowledge it and ask God to forgive you. When you pray and ask God to forgive you of your sins, He does. Completely. Now you are free to face your marriage with a clean slate on your end. This really helps to see things clearly and make the necessary adjustments to your attitude of expectations. Plus, going to God and confessing to Him creates harmony in your heart, which in turn benefits your marriage abundantly.

Forever seems like for-ev-er! It's not. We are here on earth for a blink of an eye. God is looking at us with eternity in His heart, knowing that is where we are headed. "For he knows our frame, he remembers that we are dust" (Psalm 103:14). Do you want your life—your wisp of wind—to be one that leaves a pleasing aroma or that skunk smell of expectations? You have the will to choose. God gave us free wills to worship Him. Choose wisely. Your choices will affect not only your husband but the family around you.

The blessing of being married for the long term is that it affects you in a positive way. Enjoying the benefits of marriage every day is extremely beneficial to your mental health and your physical health. Don't expect marriage to be a cookie cutter that you designed. You need each other to get the daily chores done and to give each other intimate hugs. Being together in marriage is a visual display of God's love. You have each other to hold, so hold on tight!

The sharing of a life together creates such beauty. The whole picture of marriage is like the painting of a landscape that draws you in. If your marriage doesn't seem like an extraordinary masterpiece, then turn to God. "Is anything too hard for the Lord?" (Genesis 18:14). Nothing is too hard for God. He can and will turn your marriage into a radiant portrait when you trust in Him. That family picture on the wall is a display of God's creativity and love. See the beauty in your marriage and dust off the frame.

That old saying "ball and chain" comes from an attitude of restriction rather than an attitude of attachment. Marriage was meant to be enjoyed together and add to our lives here on earth. You might feel attached at the hip, but truly you need your husband to lean on. Think of the support you can give and receive from each other. Just like two magnets. Polar opposites attract, and that magnetism is the strength you need for the long term. Lean into each other and appreciate the attraction.

The words "older" and "wiser" seem to have negative connotations but not from the Lord's point of view. "Gray hair is a crown of glory; it is gained in a righteous life. Whoever is slow to anger is better than the mighty and he who rules his spirit than he who takes a city" (Proverbs 16:31–32). Grow in gray hair together. It's your crown of glory. Rule your spirit so that the ugliness of expectations doesn't pop out. A righteous marriage is one that honors the Lord first. Grow old together living out your best life with Jesus.

I love my husband, and I know he loves me probably more than I love him. A lifetime married to him sounds pretty amazing to me. The comfort and stability of knowing we both have a relationship with Jesus first and then each other brings such peace to my soul. His spontaneous nature mixed with my need for plans on the calendar have made for a fun mix in our marriage. He has yet to answer a direct question, but his hilarious responses to the circumstances in our lives have always made me smile from the inside out. I'm expecting to giggle with him until death parts us, and then we'll have eternity to look forward to.

Conclusion

Expectations in marriage are not biblical, and they are not from the Lord. They need to leave your house, your room, and your mind. Give them to Jesus. He can meet those needs with His perfect timing in everything. Love is the glue between you and your husband. Love each other with the joy of the Lord bursting from your heart. Pour that overflowing love and respect onto your husband, and soak in the blessings.

Here are a few nuggets of wisdom from my long-married friends and family for a fulfilling life with your husband. Just remember that sometimes the small things make the biggest difference.

*S*tay in the game.

*M*ake time for romance.

*A*lways hold hands when you walk.

*L*ove spending time together.

*L*ove each other, faults and all!

Printed in the United States
by Baker & Taylor Publisher Services